THE PILGRIMS: BRAVE SETTLERS OF PLYMOUTH

stood alone against a vast wilderness and conquered it. How they managed to shelter themselves, to wrest their food from the forest, the fields, and the sea—how they managed to survive at all—is a story of courage almost beyond belief. The Pilgrims are part of a heritage of which America can well be proud. Less sturdy settlers might never have found the strength to endure such grueling experiences.

The leader of the Pilgrims, Governor William Bradford, kept a journal in which he told of their struggles and hardships, their achievements in spite of staggering odds, until they were at last "standing on their owne leggs." Bradford's journal provided much of the authentic factual material for this fascinating story. The Pilgrims come to life as real people—people who made a dream come true. Old prints, engravings, and fresh color illustrations highlight the text.

How They Lived books have been carefully planned to give greater meaning to the study of American history. Young readers will develop deeper understanding and appreciation of the brave beginnings of our nation as they see the past through the eyes of the people who lived it.

The Pilgrims: Brave Settlers of Plymouth

The Pilgrims

Brave Settlers of Plymouth

BY LYNN GROH

ILLUSTRATED BY FRANK VAUGHN

GARRARD PUBLISHING COMPANY
CHAMPAIGN, ILLINOIS

Especially for Barbara

Picture credits:

Folger Shakespeare Library: p. 26

Local History Division, New York Public Library: p. 1, 5, 13, 29, 38, 41, 43, 65, 67, 88, back cover

Museum of the American Indian, Heye Foundation: p. 87

New York Historical Society: p. 2–3

Picture Collection, New York Public Library: p. 15, 48, 81

Pilgrim Hall: p. 21, 31, 34–35, 36, 63, 68, 74, 75, 78, 90

Plimoth Plantation: p. 8–9, 18, 22, 27, 92

Endsheets: *Landing of the Pilgrims*
Courtesy of
Mrs. Robert B. Bowles,
Plymouth, Massachusetts

Contents

1. A Clearing in the Wilderness . . 7
2. Homes for a Hopeful People . . . 15
3. Day of Rest 28
4. A Long Walk to Market 38
5. Toil and Trouble 48
6. City Folks in the Country . . . 58
7. First Lady of Plymouth Plantation 67
8. The First Taste of Sweetness . . 79
9. Mother Plymouth 88
   Glossary 93
   Index 94

1. A Clearing in the Wilderness

BOOM . . . BOOM . . . BOOM!

The lookout fired three warning shots from a cannon on a hill overlooking the tiny English settlement called Plymouth Plantation. Echoes rang through the woods and meadows, shattering the quiet of the lonely wilderness.

At the sound of the cannon, children on the beaches left the buckets holding clams they had dug and ran home. Woodcutters dropped their axes in the forests and rushed back to the village.

What could be wrong? Was there a fire? Had someone been hurt? Were Indians threatening to attack the settlement?

"A ship! A ship is coming!" someone shouted.

A messenger from Indian friends on Cape Cod had run to the village with the news. The Indians had seen the tall white sails of a ship drawing near the Cape, headed for Plymouth.

Excitedly the little band of settlers milled about in the one dirt road of the settlement, called only The Street. They all talked at once.

"Is it English?"

"Could it be French pirates?"

The date was November 21, 1621. At that

These small frame houses huddled close to the harbor were all that could be seen from the sea.

time England and France were enemies. French ships carrying fur traders to Canada sometimes attacked and robbed English ships at sea. The settlers feared that pirates from the French ships might raid Plymouth, too. They had to be ready for friends or enemies.

Quickly Captain Miles Standish, the military leader of Plymouth, sent some of the men to join the lookout on the hill. They would man the three cannons that stood there with muzzles pointed over the harbor. Captain Standish made sure that all the men had guns. And he

gave a gun to every boy who was strong enough to hold the long-barreled muskets.

The settlers crowded into the seven small, crude houses scattered along The Street. The men barred the doors and stood by the windows, guns ready. The women banked the fires in the fireplaces so that no smoke would rise from the chimneys. Then they gathered the children about them.

Anxiously the settlers waited to see what the ship would bring. There were only 52 people living in Plymouth: 16 men, 8 women, and 28 children. And they were alone in the wilderness, with no one to call on for help.

Finally the ship, the *Fortune*, sailed into Plymouth harbor and ran up her colors—the white flag with the red cross of England.

Still the settlers waited. Pirates might use false colors to deceive their victims until the last minute.

Aboard the *Fortune*, 35 passengers waited as anxiously as the settlers. They had come from England to join the "planters," as the Plymouth settlers were called. The long voyage had been a merry one, despite the crowded, uncomfortable ship. Most of the passengers were strong, adventurous young men, looking for excitement in the New World. Perhaps they would find a fortune, too.

But their merrymaking ended when they neared land and saw for the first time the wintry New England coast. There was no sign of life. Even when the ship sailed into Plymouth harbor, the men could see only a row of tiny cottages. No one moved on the dirt road. The village was as still as death.

Were all the planters dead? Had they been carried off by Indians?

"You can't leave us here!" the passengers cried. "Take us back to England!"

"We don't have enough food for you to eat on the way back," some of the crew argued. "This is where we were hired to bring you, and here you will stay. When you go ashore, we will sail for home."

"We will take your sails ashore with us!" cried one of the men. "Then you can't sail without us." Twenty-six strong young men rushed to the masts to take down the sails. The crew tried to push them back.

The captain hurried on deck to stop the fight. He promised the passengers that if they found no one at Plymouth he would take them south to Virginia, where there was another English colony.

The captain himself rowed ashore in a long-boat with some of the men. There was still no one in sight when they tied up at a landing at the foot of the dirt road. Then the cottage doors opened, and the people came out. The newcomers gave a wild cheer. The planters were alive!

Joyfully the planters rushed down The Street, eager to greet the passengers from the *Fortune* and to get news of England.

The Mayflower rides at anchor in Plymouth Harbor as the Pilgrims land in 1620.

More than a year had passed since these planters, whom we now call Pilgrims, had left England because they had not been allowed to worship God according to their own beliefs. The *Mayflower*, in which they had sailed, had been lent to them by a group of merchants in England. These merchants had also given them food, clothing, and tools, and had promised to send them supplies for seven years. In return the Pilgrims had agreed to ship back furs, lumber, and dried fish. But no supplies had yet come from the merchants, and the Pilgrims had endured a sad, hard time.

13

Fifty persons—mothers, fathers, and children—had died of a strange illness that they called the "General Sickness." The food that they had brought with them was gone. Although they had managed to grow enough food to keep them alive through the coming winter, they were very thin and often hungry. Their clothes were ragged, and they needed many things. Now surely the *Fortune* had brought some of these things.

But the *Fortune* had brought them nothing. The merchants had not even sent supplies for the 35 newcomers.

The leader of the Pilgrims, Governor William Bradford, kept a journal in which he told of the *Fortune*'s arrival. The journal also tells how the Pilgrims, alone and deserted by the English merchants, managed to live in the wilderness, getting their food from the forest, the fields, and the sea.

2. Homes for a Hopeful People

There were now thirty-five more people in Plymouth, and there was not room for them in the seven little houses. Some of the young bachelors built crude lean-tos of branches, or slept on the dirt floors of the two storehouses. Chill November winds warned that winter was near, however. The Pilgrims knew they must build more houses so that everyone would be sheltered from the cold.

Each morning, as soon as it was light, the men gathered at the Common House, where Governor Bradford gave them their tools. Then they went to work.

Before long The Street was filled with the
sounds of busy people. Laughing boys raced
each other up the hill from the spring, carrying big wooden buckets filled with water. A
band of children, bundled in shawls and stock-
ing caps, set out for the beach to find clams
and mussels for the noon meal.

From the dooryards came a steady, rhythmic
beat: *Thump* . . . *thump* . . . *thump* . . .
thump. . . . Women were pounding corn into
meal as the Indians did, by patiently dropping

16

a heavy stone against the grain, held in a hollowed-out log.

But the sounds of axes, hammers, and saws were heard above all else. Some men worked at the sawpit, sawing great tree trunks into boards. Others put up heavy oak frames for the houses.

Teams of woodcutters kept the builders well supplied with fresh logs from the forest. The Pilgrims had no horses or oxen, so the heavy loads had to be carried, or dragged with ropes to the village.

The houses were to be lined up in neat rows on either side of The Street. Except for size, all would be very much alike. Each would have one large room, with a sleeping loft overhead, reached by a ladder. The floor was the ground, with the dirt packed down until it was almost as hard as stone.

A huge fireplace would fill one wall of the room. The first houses in Plymouth colony had fireplaces and flues made of green saplings. Because these fireplaces often caught on fire, some of the new houses would have stone fireplaces. The men gathered great piles of stones

Clapboard walls and thatched roofs reminded Pilgrims of the homes they had left behind in England.

from the fields and meadows nearby. They were of many odd shapes and sizes and would be fitted together like the pieces of a jigsaw puzzle to make fireplaces and chimneys.

Building was slow because each board had to be sawed, trimmed, and smoothed by hand. Even the wooden nails—called "treenails" but pronounced "trunnels" by the English—had to be carved by hand.

Each day the men worked until it was too dark to see. Then they returned their crude axes, saws, and planes to the Common House. Even then, some men continued working by the flickering light of candles or pine knots. They carved nails, fitted oiled paper into wooden frames for the windows, and tied rushes into tight bundles to be used for the thatched roofs.

Twenty-two-year-old John Alden was eager to finish his house for a special reason. He was engaged, and would be married as soon as he had a home for his bride. His would be one of the smallest houses in Plymouth, but it would be as fine as any house he could have owned in England.

John had been a poor cooper, or barrelmaker, in Harwich, England. He could not always find work, and when he did, the hours were long and the pay was poor. It would have taken him many years to earn enough money to marry, and he might never have owned a home. When he heard that the Pilgrims wanted to hire a cooper for the *Mayflower*'s voyage to America, he thought the sailing trip sounded like a great adventure, so he took the job.

John liked the Pilgrims. He admired their kindness to each other. He especially liked the fact that they elected their own leaders, and every man voted for the rules by which they lived. The future looked bright in this wild New World. There was land to be had by clearing it. Trees waited to be cut and made into houses. John had decided to stay. He was "a hopeful young man," Governor Bradford wrote in his journal, and the Pilgrims welcomed him as a planter of Plymouth Plantation.

Priscilla Mullins was still another reason why John Alden had stayed. We know little about Priscilla, except that she was nineteen, and an orphan. Her father, mother, and brother had all died in the General Sickness. Priscilla was now the ward of Ruling Elder William Brewster, the Pilgrims' religious leader, who took care of several Pilgrim orphans.

Elder Brewster had given John and Priscilla

The Mayflower Compact which was signed by most Pilgrims promised the colonists "just & equall lawes."

permission to marry. And when John finished their house, Priscilla planned to take to it the bedding, linen, pots, and pans that her parents had brought to Plymouth.

But their plans had to wait. Late in November, a messenger from Chief Canonicus of the Narragansett Indians came to Plymouth. He handed Governor Bradford a sheaf of arrows wrapped in a rattlesnake skin. The Pilgrims' Indian friend, Squanto, told them that this was a challenge to war.

The Pilgrims were alarmed. How could so few of them fight a whole tribe of Indians? Governor Bradford, thinking it was wise not to

A Drawing of Plymouth Colony

1. The Street	3. The Fort	5. The Cornfields
2. The Highway	4. The Wall	6. The Brook

show their terror, wrapped some bullets in the same snakeskin and sent it back to Chief Canonicus. Now the chief was alarmed. He would not touch the snakeskin, but sent it on from one tribe to another until, finally, a messenger brought it back to Plymouth. This meant that the Narragansetts would not attack, at least for the moment.

Still, Canonicus was the enemy of another Indian friend of the Pilgrims, Chief Massasoit, of the Wampanoags. Since Canonicus could not be trusted, the Pilgrims decided that they needed more protection.

All other work was stopped while the men began to build a wall of saplings, called palings, all around the village. The palings were about eleven feet high and were cut to a sharp point at the top. They were set in the ground tightly pressed together, so there were only narrow cracks between them.

Hundreds of saplings had to be cut and dragged in from the forest. There was no rest for the men, except on Sunday. On Christmas Day Governor Bradford called them to work as usual. The Pilgrims did not celebrate Christmas, because they thought it was a pagan custom. Many of the newcomers who had arrived on the *Fortune*, though, did observe Christmas. They said "it was against their conscience" to work.

Governor Bradford agreed that these men need not work that day. When he came back from the forest later, however, he found the newcomers in The Street playing games like stool ball and pitching the bar.

"It is against my conscience for you to play while others work," Governor Bradford said, and he sent them indoors.

The men labored all winter, and when spring came the wall was finished. Then one day a boat arrived at Plymouth bringing a letter that contained alarming news. The letter was from a Captain Huddleston, who was with an English fleet that was fishing off the coast of Maine, 150 miles away. It told of an Indian uprising in the Virginia Colony. Three hundred and forty-seven of the English settlers had been massacred.

Could such a thing happen at Plymouth? Captain Standish said they needed a fort as well as the wall they had just finished. Wearily the men began dragging great oak trees to the top of the hill where their cannons stood. They should have been tending their crops.

Food was so low that the Pilgrims were living on half rations. The men were so weak from hunger they could hardly handle the big trees.

Although they were badly needed to work on the fort, young Edward Winslow and two other men were sent to try to find the English fishing fleet. Perhaps the ships had food to spare. This was a dangerous journey because the Pilgrims' little shallop, a small open boat, was not built for sea voyages, and the men had never been to Maine. They might never

The armor of this seventeenth century musketeer is
much like the armor worn by Pilgrim soldiers.

return. Still, the Pilgrims must have more food
soon, or die.

Late in the summer of 1622 the fort was
finished. It was one large room, with walls so
thick that even a cannonball would not go
through them. The roof was a flat, walled
platform with openings for the cannon muzzles.
The Pilgrims were proud of their new building,

26

the grandest one in Plymouth. They used it for church services and town meetings.

They felt safe from the Indians. Now they waited anxiously for Edward Winslow's return, so they might also be safe from starvation.

Somehow, in spite of all the hard work, John Alden found time to finish his house. We do not know the exact date, but sometime in 1622 John and Priscilla were married. They moved into the little house, next door to Captain Standish at the foot of Fort Hill, to start a new family in Plymouth.

A helmeted soldier patrols the roof of the new fort.

3. Day of Rest

Fourteen-year-old Thomas Cushman stood before Captain Standish's house and proudly beat
on a drum. People came from every house and
formed a line along The Street. It was eight
o'clock on a Sunday morning, and the Pilgrims
were going to church in their new meetinghouse in the fort.

Thomas could feel the other boys watching
him enviously, but he kept his eyes straight
ahead. He beat the drum hard until the last
stragglers were in line.

A soldier marched smartly into position at

the head of the line to lead the way. Behind him came the three Pilgrim leaders, Governor Bradford in the center, with Elder Brewster on his right, and Captain Standish on his left.

The rest of the people followed, in three lines, with women and children walking in the middle line. The men, carrying their muskets, were on the outside. Even at worship the Pilgrims had to be prepared for a surprise attack by Indians. The people exchanged polite greetings, but no one stopped to talk. Their Sabbath had started at sundown the day before, and there could be no idle chatter until the Sabbath ended at sundown on Sunday.

Thomas put away the drum, got his own musket, and joined the long line. Solemnly the Pilgrims marched up the hill to the fort. They were dressed in their best clothes, but after almost two years without any new garments, their best was rather poor.

The "sad," or dark, shades of blue, green, red, and brown of the women's dresses were so faded that the garments scarcely had any color at all. The long skirts, which reached to the ankles, were frayed at the bottom and had great patches where torn places had been mended.

The men's knee breeches were also patched, some with pieces of soft deerskin. Sleeves were torn from shirts, and most of the Pilgrims wore battered shoes without stockings.

Little girls dressed just like their mothers, and boys under six years wore a dresslike frock called a coat. The growing children's clothes had been lengthened so often now that usually there was no hem left, and little wrists stuck far out of sleeves that had become far too short.

The Pilgrims did not think of staying home from church because they had no nice clothes. The marchers filed into the big room of the fort and took their seats on long wooden benches. Every person in Plymouth Plantation was present, except for one man. He was the lookout posted above on the roof of the fort. His steady tramp, tramp, tramping back and forth overhead could be heard throughout the long service.

The men sat on one side of the room, the women on the other. The children sat in the rear, by themselves. They were watched over by Dr. Samuel Fuller, the church deacon, who kept order in the church. He had a long birch

Even very young children came to the first religious service held by the Pilgrims in the New World.

rod with a bone knob at the end. If a child misbehaved, Deacon Fuller tapped him smartly on the head with the rod. If a grown-up dared to nod during the sermon, he also got a rap on the head.

Statues, pictures, and other decorations were forbidden in the Pilgrim meetinghouse. Nor were any musical instruments permitted. When the Pilgrims stood to sing an opening hymn, someone who had a good voice "set the pitch," and the others joined in.

Since there was no pulpit, Elder Brewster stood behind a plain wooden table to conduct the service. He began with a prayer that lasted an hour or longer. He prayed for food, for protection from the Indians, and for friends who were still in England, waiting for the English merchants to send them to America as they had promised to do.

Thomas Cushman might have added a silent prayer of his own because his father, Deacon Robert Cushman, was still in London. They had arrived in Plymouth on the *Fortune*, but Deacon Cushman had returned immediately on the ship to try to get supplies for the hungry Pilgrims. Unhappily, Thomas' prayers were not answered. Deacon Cushman died of a plague in London, and Thomas was left as one of many Pilgrim orphans. He was adopted by his father's friend, Governor Bradford.

After the prayer Elder Brewster preached for about two hours. The summer sun beat down upon the roof. Little fresh air came through the small windows, and the fort became stiflingly hot. The log benches had no backs to lean against, and the Pilgrims had to sit up straight, through the long, hot morning.

In winter, when snow lay deep on the ground and icy winds whistled about the fort, the people shivered through the long service. They wrapped themselves in extra shawls and covered their feet and legs with woolen lap rugs. A few had warming pans filled with live coals on which they rested their feet to keep them warm. The Pilgrims suffered especially from cold feet because their stockings were only leggings, with a loop under the foot to keep them in place. Inside their shoes, the Pilgrims' feet were bare.

At noon the Pilgrims left the meetinghouse as solemnly as they had entered it, and they remained solemn for the rest of the day. Work of any kind was forbidden. Food had been prepared the day before. In winter, when a

fire was needed for warmth, they were allowed
to warm their food in the big iron pots that
hung directly over the flames. In summer,
Sunday dinner was served cold.

In that summer of 1622, while they waited
for harvest, the Pilgrims were lucky to have a
thin bean porridge, or succotash made with
beans and corn. There was no bread, and only
water to drink. Yet the meal was served on a
clean tablecloth, to show respect for these
precious gifts from God.

After dinner some boys were sent to keep

The first Thanksgiving feast was held soon after the harvest of Fall, 1621 when food was plentiful.

birds out of the cornfields, and a lookout stood watch at the fort. Everyone else stayed quietly at home. Pilgrims who did not observe the Sabbath reverently were punished. A man and wife once had to pay a fine for quarreling on Sunday. Another man was scolded before all of the people at church because he wrote a letter before sundown.

Thomas Cushman probably received religious instruction from Elder Brewster. There was no

This Bible, treasured by Governor Bradford, lists the
birthdays of members of his family.

school in Plymouth. Yet the Pilgrims knew
that they must have educated leaders for the
future, so Thomas and a few other boys were
given lessons by Elder Brewster, Governor
Bradford, and Dr. Fuller. Years later, when
Elder Brewster died, Thomas became the Ruling
Elder of Plymouth.

Late in the afternoon the Pilgrims went to
the fort for another long meeting. Men of the
congregation discussed a religious question. The
Pilgrims believed in the "Congregational Way,"

in which every man was free to give his own opinion. Women and children sat and listened. They were not allowed to speak in church.

Women did talk on Sunday evening. When the sun set and the Sabbath ended, visiting was permitted. The sick could always expect calls from their friends, who often sang hymns, said prayers, and read from the Bible at their bedside. Friends also visited others in need of comfort, like young Mrs. Winslow, who lived in fear while her husband Edward was away. He had not yet returned from his dangerous voyage to Maine in search of the English fishing fleet.

Danger was always present in the New World, but through their day of rest and worship, the Pilgrims found the strength to face it.

4. A Long Walk to Market

Edward Winslow and his companions at last returned from Maine. They found the Pilgrims staggering from hunger. The friendly fishing captains had given Winslow all the food they could spare, but it was mainly the hard sea biscuits that ships carried in those days.

To make the bread last until harvest, each person was allowed one pound a day. It was kept in the Common House and handed out daily to all the people. "Otherwise," Governor Bradford wrote, "had it been in their own custody, they would have eat it up & then starved."

Their crops, which had been neglected while the men built the fort, were not doing well, and harvest was still weeks away. The Pilgrims now prayed earnestly that a ship would arrive before the sea biscuits were gone. They were not hopeful, however, because they now believed that the English merchants had deserted them.

Then, early in July, the lookout shouted out joyful news. He had sighted the sails of not one, but two English ships!

But the big *Charity* and the smaller *Swan* were another disappointment. They soon arrived with 60 more men but with no supplies for the Pilgrims.

English merchants had sent these men to build a trading post at Wessagusset, on what is now called Boston Bay. The newcomers did not bring families to start a settlement, but were to spend their time cutting lumber and trading trinkets for furs with the Indians. The *Charity* had to take some other passengers south to Virginia, and the *Swan* was too small to carry the 60 men and their supplies to Boston Bay. The merchants expected the Pilgrims to provide food and shelter for these men until the *Charity* returned.

The Pilgrims thought this was unfair, but

they could not turn the men out to starve in the wilderness. The men built themselves crude shelters made of branches, and the Pilgrims fed them.

The visitors repaid this kindness by stealing corn from the fields while it was still green. They were joined in this theft, Governor Bradford wrote, by several of the hungry Pilgrims "whom conscience did not restrain." Anyone caught stealing corn was whipped.

It was a happy day for the Pilgrims when, two months later, the *Charity* returned to take the rowdy visitors to Wessagusset.

Harvest came, but there was still not nearly enough corn to last the winter. Governor Bradford feared that the Pilgrims were doomed. They could not even buy food from friendly Indians because they had no "trading commodities."

"Trading commodities" were the beads and other trinkets brought from England to use in trading with the Indians. The Pilgrims had traded all their trinkets for furs to send to the English merchants. They had none left to trade for food.

At this darkest moment, some help came unexpectedly. An English ship, the *Discovery*,

which was exploring the shores of the New
World, stopped at Plymouth. The captain had
no food to spare, but he did have a good supply
of trinkets that he wanted to trade for furs.

Eagerly the Pilgrims brought out some of
the furs they had been planning to send to
England. The greedy captain, seeing that they
were starving, offered them only a few strings
of beads for the finest furs. The Pilgrims had
to accept the price or face starvation.

Governor Bradford immediately left Plymouth
on a trading trip. The Pilgrims' shallop was
too small to carry the winter's supply of food

he hoped to buy, so he went first to Wessagusset. He made an agreement with the traders there. They would supply their ship, the *Swan*, and a crew; the Pilgrims would supply the trinkets and their shallop; and the two groups would share the food they bought.

With the shallop tied behind the *Swan*, and with the Pilgrims' friend Squanto as interpreter, the traders set out. The stormy season was beginning as they sailed along the coast of Cape Cod. The little ships were so tossed by wind and waves that they were forced to find shelter at the Indian village of Monomoy, now called Chatham.

There the saddest of several misfortunes befell them. Squanto suddenly fell ill of a raging fever. Governor Bradford bathed his friend and gave him broths made of herbs. Nothing helped. Two days later Squanto died, Governor Bradford reported, "asking the Governor to pray for him, that he might go to the Englishmen's God in heaven." Squanto would be sorely missed for he had been the Pilgrims' teacher and their interpreter in dealing with the Indians.

The traders had to go on. They had collected about 20 hogsheads of corn and beans when they reached Nauset, north of Monomoy. There they bought ten hogsheads of corn from the Indians, but before they could load it, a violent storm arose. The shallop broke loose from the bigger ship and sank. The *Swan* could not sail into the shallow water near shore to be loaded, so the corn had to be left until workers could return to raise the shallop.

The Wessagusset men sailed home in the *Swan*, stopping first at Plymouth to leave the Pilgrims' share of the food. Governor Bradford and the Pilgrim group walked home, a distance of about 50 miles. At Plymouth the governor arranged for Captain Standish to take workers to raise the shallop. Then he went on to some

Governor Bradford's search for food took him to the tents and campfires of neighboring Indian villages.

inland villages. He walked some fifteen miles to Nemasket, where he bought several bushels of corn and hired Indian squaws to carry the corn to Plymouth.

His next stop was an Indian settlement on the Manomet River at a place now included in the township of Sandwich on Cape Cod. The friendly Cape Indians sold him several hogsheads of corn, beans, and dried berries. These also had to be left until the shallop was repaired.

A weary Governor Bradford returned at last to Plymouth, his marketing done for the winter. He had braved storms at sea and had walked well over 100 miles along rough Indian trails. Captain Standish's men finally raised the shallop and brought the food that had been left behind. Then the Governor knew that by living on half rations, the Pilgrims could survive until spring.

The men selected several bushels of the best corn to save for seed. Perhaps they buried this corn in woven baskets covered with straw mats, as the Indians did, to keep it safe from fire and from mice and other pests. Then the night guard would have kept special watch over it. No matter how hungry anyone might be, no one must be allowed to touch the precious

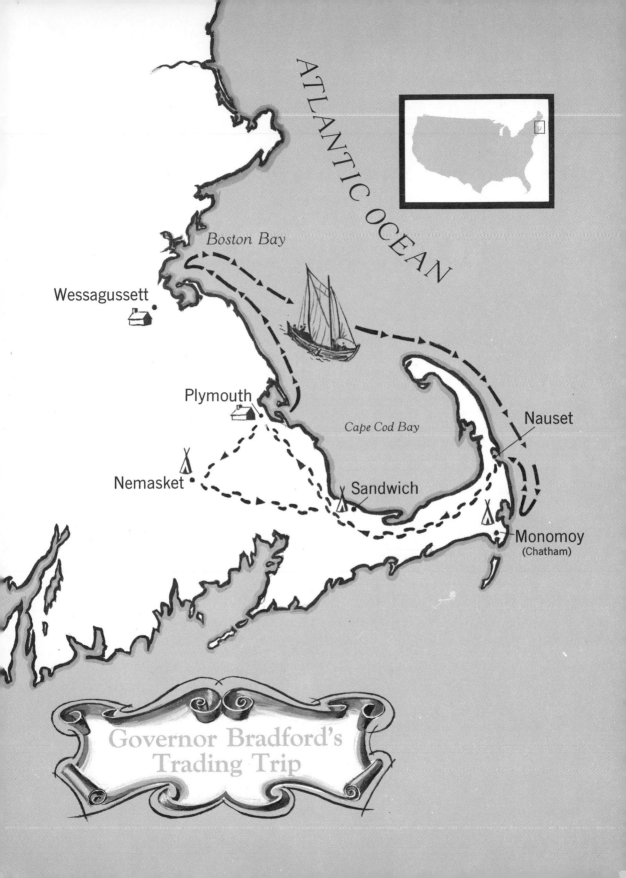

ATLANTIC OCEAN

Boston Bay

Wessagussett

Plymouth

Cape Cod Bay

Nauset

Nemasket

Sandwich

Monomoy
(Chatham)

Governor Bradford's
Trading Trip

seed corn. The Pilgrims would need to plant it in the spring if they were to eat in the coming year.

As the men worked, the Governor heard some of them grumbling about shirkers and laws that were unfair. He knew that they were talking about the Pilgrims' system of farming, which was called "communal." The merchants in England had ordered them to follow this system until they had paid in furs, lumber, and fish for the use of the *Mayflower* and for supplies.

In the communal system the land and even the tools were owned by the whole community and not by individuals. Everyone was expected to do an equal share of the work and everyone shared equally in the crops.

But not everyone did his fair share, and shirkers were given as much food from the common store as the men who worked hard. Governor Bradford thought this was unjust. He believed that everyone would work if he was working for himself. Yet the Governor had no right to change the system.

As winter wore on the food supplies became lower and daily rations had to be cut. The grumbling became louder and there were open quarrels among the Pilgrims. Governor Bradford was worried about them. They were turning against each other just when they most needed to stand together. They now knew that they could not count on supplies from England. They must plant bigger fields, tend their crops more carefully, and feed themselves—or go hungry.

Still, the Governor had faith in the courage and good will of his people. He believed that when spring came, with its promise of new life and new hope, they would meet together and find a way to live peacefully again.

5. Toil and Trouble

Governor Bradford rapped sharply on the wooden table in front of him. Gradually the babble of voices quieted and the Pilgrims came to order. It was March 25, 1623, and they were holding their annual Town Meeting at the fort.

It was also the Pilgrims' New Year's Day, because they followed the Old Style calendar then used in England. New Year's Day was the only legal holiday the Pilgrims observed. The day began with the Town Meeting, at which they elected their leaders for another year and discussed the colony's problems. The rest of the day was celebrated by feasting, when there was enough food, and in visiting and playing games.

In 1623 celebrating was far from the Pilgrims' minds. They quickly re-elected William Bradford as their governor, and Isaac Allerton as his assistant. Then they all began to talk at once about the question that concerned them most—the food shortage. All the Pilgrims were now certain that their communal system of farming was to blame for their poor crops.

Each man believed he could grow better crops if he had his own farm and worked alone. Governor Bradford knew that there would soon be real trouble unless the system was changed. The English merchants who had made the rule were safe in their comfortable homes in London. How could they know what was best for the planters in Plymouth?

Wisely the Governor decided to disobey the merchants and to assign each family or household a farm of its own. Food from hunting and fishing would still be shared equally, but each household would keep for itself all the crops grown on its farm.

Each farm contained one acre for each member of the household. John and Priscilla Alden were given two acres. Edward Winslow

was assigned eight acres, because his household included his wife, two stepsons, two younger brothers, his brother-in-law, and a servant. And so it went.

Now that he had his own field to plant, each man was eager to start working. About the middle of April, the buds on the trees opened. At this sign all the men went into their fields outside the village wall to prepare the ground for seed. They had no plows, nor animals to pull them. With crude iron mattocks and hoes and with wooden spades, they turned the hard earth and chopped it into fine soil. They raked away stones and pebbles.

Meantime, at each high tide, the children kept watch at the brook. Squanto had taught the Pilgrims that the best fertilizer for the stony soil at Plymouth was made of the herring that came into the brook near the end of April. These fish usually live in the sea, but when spring comes they look for quiet inland streams where they lay their eggs so the young can hatch in calm water.

The first child to see a herring in the brook gave a joyful cry that brought all the Pilgrims running to watch the fish arrive. As usual the herring poured into the brook in such large numbers that they actually bumped into each

other. The fish could be seen clearly in the shallow brook, which in some places was no more than a foot deep. The children piled stones across the stream, then squealed with delight as the determined herring leaped and tumbled over the barrier. They could not be turned back.

Squanto had helped the Pilgrims build a weir, or fence, across the mouth of the brook. A gate in the center was opened at high tide to let the herring in. When enough fish had entered the trap, the door was closed. Farther upstream another weir kept the herring in the enclosure.

Now the men dug up the baskets of precious seed corn that had been guarded all winter. Each family was given a share of the seed, according to the size of its farm, and everyone worked. The women and children carried their hoes and spades to the fields to plant the seed. The men and older boys trudged back and forth to the brook, scooping up herring in woven baskets and wooden kegs and carrying them to the fields.

The Pilgrims planted their corn in hills about four feet apart. They dug a hole into which they dropped three herring, heads together and

tails spread out like the spokes of a wheel. A thin layer of earth was spread over the fish. Then the children dropped in a few grains of the red, blue, purple, and yellow Indian corn.

Someone made a rhyme about the number of seed to be used in each hill:

Five kernels of corn in a row:
One for the blackbird, one for the crow,
One for the cutworm, and two to grow!

The herring run lasted about three weeks. All the planting had to be done before it ended, because without fish for fertilizer the corn would not grow. The work was not equal, of course, for some households had several grown men to help, while others had only small children. Still, the Pilgrims were happy. In his journal Governor Bradford reported on the new system of family farming:

"This had very good success, for it made all hands very industrious, so as much more corn was planted than otherwise would have been."

The work did not end with planting corn.

Afterward the Pilgrims planted beans in each corn hill. When the bean vines grew, they would twine around the cornstalks. Pumpkins and squash were planted between the rows of corn. Their vines would spread out, shading the ground to help keep weeds from growing.

Soon the fish in the corn hills began to have a very strong smell. This caused hungry wolves to gather in the woods nearby. They hid in the daytime but slipped into the fields at night to dig up the herring. The Pilgrims piled brush around the fields and, at night, set great bonfires to frighten the wolves away.

The men and older boys took turns standing watch, keeping the huge bonfires burning, and shooting the squirrels, rabbits, and woodchucks that came at night to eat the tender plants. Teams of boys spent their days chasing away blackbirds and crows that swooped down to scratch up the seed or pull up the young blades.

But the worst enemy of the corn was the sly cutworm. During the day the cutworms hid in the earth at the roots of the corn. At night they crawled out to eat, chewing through the stalk just above the ground. Then the stalk fell over like a tree that has been cut down with an ax.

Squanto had shown the children how to dig gently around the roots to find the worms. The children killed them with sticks or stones.

Besides the cutworms and other pests, there was also a drought in that summer of 1623. For weeks not a drop of rain fell. The cornstalks and bean vines wilted and began to turn brown and dry. It seemed that the Pilgrims' crops would die.

Governor Bradford and Elder Brewster called for "a solemn day of humiliation," when all the Pilgrims would gather in the fort to pray for rain. Edward Winslow told all about the meeting in a booklet called *Good Newes From New England:*

"In the morning, when we assembled together, the heavens were as clear, and the drought as like to continue as ever it was," Winslow wrote. Still the Pilgrims prayed on, all through the sunny, cloudless day. Eight hours passed. Then, very late in the afternoon, Winslow reported, the sky became overcast, and "the clouds gathered together on all sides."

Next morning, the Pilgrims were awakened by the sound of a soft, gentle rain falling on their roofs. It rained for fourteen days, and their withered crops turned green again.

Joyfully the Pilgrims set aside another "solemn day," this one a day of thanksgiving. The English merchants might fail them. They might know days of hunger. But the Pilgrims were convinced that their God would not forsake them.

6. City Folks in the Country

One day after the rain ended, the Pilgrims' shallop tied up at the landing and six weary men, smelling of fish, came ashore. Other men began unloading the cod, bass, and bluefish that the fishermen had caught. The catch was not large, perhaps enough to last the colony two days. It was all the fishermen had to show for five long, dangerous days at sea.

Still the Pilgrims took the fish hungrily. While their crops were growing they had little else to eat. After the seed corn was planted their storehouses were empty, Governor Bradford wrote, and they had to "rest on God's providence" to find some food each day. Usually they went to bed at night not knowing where they might be able to find "a bitt of anything the next day."

The "bitt" usually was fish. The Pilgrims had only the shallop for fishing, so the men were divided into teams to take turns going out. As soon as a catch was unloaded, a new team sailed off to the deep-sea fishing grounds.

The boat was so small that only six or seven men could go at one time. Often they stayed out at sea for several days. They took turns sleeping.

When it rained they sat shivering in the open boat. There was no cabin or any other shelter from the weather. The Pilgrims had so little food that the men took only dried berries and groundnuts with them. They ate some of the fish they caught, cooking it over an open fire built in a box of sand.

The Pilgrims had never fished before coming to America, and they really did not know how. They had even brought the wrong fishing gear.

Their nets were small and weak, made for catching little fish. The big cod and bluefish sometimes broke the nets and got away. Then the men had to stop and mend the nets before they could put them out again.

They also fished with hand lines and hooks. But their hooks were so big that fish often stole the bait without being caught. Still, the fishermen kept trying. Governor Bradford said:

"Neither did they return till they had caught something, though it were five or six days before. For they knew there was nothing at home, and to go home empty would be a great discouragement to the rest."

Sometimes the men did not catch enough fish and everyone had to look for shellfish on the beach at low tide. Men, women, and children went barefoot along the beach to find the shellfish—clams, mussels, and sea snails. Instead of building a hot fire in the house fireplace in summer, the Pilgrims might have had a clambake on the beach as the Indians had taught them.

First they would dig a hole in the sand and line it with stones. A hot fire was built on the stones and left for several hours until the stones were heated through. The embers were then raked away and the stones covered with rockweed. All of the shellfish were tossed in together and covered well with more rockweed, topped by green branches. The heat from the stones and the moisture from the rockweed steamed the shellfish until they were juicy and tender.

Many people have clambakes today, but not day after day as the Pilgrims sometimes did. Governor Bradford said they only had a change of diet now and then when someone shot a deer, "for one or two of the fittest was appointed to range the woods for that end."

Even "the fittest" Pilgrims were poor hunters, for all of them had been townspeople before coming to Plymouth, and were not trained in hunting or even in using guns. They had not known what animals they would find in the New World.

The first two men who went hunting, not long after the Pilgrims had arrived on the *Mayflower*, got lost in the woods. Darkness came and a heavy snow began to fall. Suddenly the men heard a frightening noise, which later they described as "two lions roaring exceedingly, for a long time together." All that night they huddled under a tree, ready to climb it if they were attacked. When morning came they found their way home.

Later while walking in the woods, one of the men heard the same noise again. This time two wild animals leaped out of the bushes and ran away. But they were not lions, they were wolves. The Pilgrims had a good laugh at the hunters who did not know a wolf from a lion.

But there was little joking now when hunters went to find food for empty tables. In summer all the birds and many of the deer moved to northern feeding grounds. The men walked long distances to wait at watering places and feeding grounds for deer to appear.

Their crude muskets had very long barrels. When shooting, the men rested the barrels on a stand, usually a forked stick set in the ground. A hunter had to hit his target with the first shot, because it took several minutes to put a new bullet into the gun, stuff in the

This musket, used by Pilgrims to hunt, was fired by means of a slowly burning fuse.

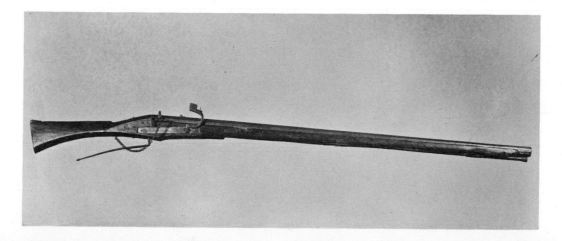

wadding, and pour powder into the powder pan. By that time all the wild creatures had scurried to safety.

On lucky days the hunters returned with one or two deer slung by their feet on a long pole that the hunters carried between them. Eighty-five hungry Pilgrims soon finished the deer meat, called venison. Then they ate fish again.

The Pilgrims' health suffered from the poor diet. They knew nothing of dental care, so when cavities in their teeth developed, they had no way of filling them. When bad teeth had to be pulled, the unfortunate Pilgrim had to live on foods that did not have to be chewed.

With their gaunt appearance and shabby clothes, the poor Pilgrims looked like outcasts. Certainly they were not prepared to receive company. But company did come. The *Anne* arrived first, and about two weeks later came the *Little James*. The two ships brought 93 new people to Plymouth.

It was a happy time for many Pilgrims whose loved ones finally joined them. Elder Brewster and his wife were reunited with their two daughters, Patience and Fear. The wife and five daughters of Richard Warren arrived, along with many others.

The Pilgrims had little to offer the newcomers.

"The best dish they could presente their friends with was a lobster, or a peece of fish, without bread, or anything else but a cupp of fair spring water," Governor Bradford wrote. He was also embarrassed at the clothes worn by his people, some of whom were "little better than half naked."

As for the newcomers, they were horrified at the ragged condition of the Pilgrims. Some of them, Governor Bradford reported, "fell a-weeping, fancying their owne miserie in what they saw now in others."

Again, the English merchants had sent no supplies for the Pilgrims. There was scarcely enough food on the two ships to last the newcomers through the winter. There were ill feelings at once. The Pilgrims knew that their harvest would not feed everyone. For their part, the newcomers feared that the starving Pilgrims would eat all the provisions brought on the ships. Finally it was agreed that the Pilgrims would keep all their harvest, and the newcomers would have the ships' supplies.

And now the Pilgrims were busy loading the *Anne* with lumber and furs.

When she sailed for England late in August, 26-year-old Edward Winslow was aboard. This dashing young man had become the Pilgrims' best diplomat, having, as a friend said, "a silver tongue." Perhaps he would be able to persuade the English merchants to send the food and clothes and tools the Pilgrims needed so badly.

7. First Lady of Plymouth Plantation

The *Anne* and the *Little James* brought no food or clothing for the Pilgrims, but they did bring a very special addition to the colony: 27 more women to turn the crude little houses into real homes.

Among them were wives who had been left behind until the Pilgrim men could build a settlement. But there were also new brides for the men whose wives had died in Plymouth, and for the young bachelors.

Captain Standish married a young girl known only as Barbara. It is believed that Barbara

The women who arrived on the *Anne* were not as finely
dressed as this Pilgrim woman of a later date.

was the younger sister of Captain Standish's
first wife, Rose, who died in the General Sickness. Seventeen-year-old Lucretia Oldham came
to Plymouth to marry Elder Brewster's son
Jonathan. Assistant Governor Isaac Allerton soon
married Fear Brewster.

And Mrs. Alice Southworth, a widow, came
to Plymouth to become the new Mrs. Bradford.
Governor Bradford's first wife, Dorothy, had
drowned soon after the *Mayflower* arrived in
America. For three years the young Governor
had helped with the work of the colony, cared
for three orphans—and kept house for himself.

Mrs. Bradford was the First Lady of the
colony, but her daily life was just like that of
all the other wives.

Her new home in the wilderness was similar
to the peasant cottages the First Lady had
known in the English countryside. Governor
Bradford had added a room and loft to his
house, so it now consisted of the "First Room"
and loft and the "Bedchamber" and loft.

There was no bathroom, nor did the Pilgrims
have bathtubs. They believed they would get
a "temper"—their word for most illnesses—if
they undressed completely and got into a tub
of water. Instead, they bathed from a large

wooden basin—but never in plain water. They added "waters" made from certain flowers they believed to be healthful, particularly roses, which grew wild in the forests.

Eleven people may have used the same wooden basin in Governor Bradford's house. In addition to the Governor and his wife, there was his wife's sister, Mrs. Morton, and her five young children, and three orphan boys, Thomas Cushman, Joseph Rogers, and William Latham. They all lived crowded together in the two rooms and two lofts.

Cleaning such a small house took only a few minutes. Beds were merely mattresses placed on the dirt floor. Each morning the grown-ups, who slept on the first floor, rolled up their mattresses and placed them in a corner out of the way. The seven older children straightened the covers on their mattresses before climbing down the ladder from the loft where they slept. The baby, Ephraim Morton, born at sea during the voyage of the *Anne*, slept in a wooden cradle near his mother.

The dirt floor was swept with a broom made of straw or some twigs tied to a stick. Mrs. Bradford and many other Pilgrim wives had rugs, but these were considered too fine to

walk on. They were used as extra covers on cold winter nights. Later, when the Pilgrims finally got bedsteads, the rugs served as bedspreads. Smaller ones, which we would call scatter rugs, were used as table covers.

The Pilgrims at first had no sheep for wool and not enough cleared land to grow flax to make cloth. So the women could not spin and weave. Some of the *Anne* passengers had brought extra bolts of cloth, but most of the Pilgrims had only the clothes they had brought with them. The women spent their sewing time mainly patching these clothes when they tore. They called this "clouting."

An unknown Pilgrim wrote a poem about life in Plymouth. One of the verses shows that they were good-natured about their ragged clothes:

> *Our clothes we brought with us are*
> *   often much torn,*
> *They need to be clouted before they*
> *   are worn;*
> *But clouting our garments they hinder*
> *   us nothing,*
> *Clouts double, are warmer than single*
> *   whole clothing!*

Clothing was so precious in Plymouth for many years that, along with other property, the Pilgrims stated in their wills who should inherit their garments. They even included small items such as handkerchiefs, stockings, and garters.

If the weather was warm on laundry day, the First Lady went with the other wives to wash clothes in the brook. They put the clothes in the water and spanked them with wooden paddles to get them clean. This was called "bucking." The clothes were spread on clean grass, draped over bushes, or hung on garden fences to dry.

Housewives cooked their meals in huge iron pots hung over the fire in fieldstone fireplaces. Indians had introduced them to many of the new foods they used.

In the winter of 1623–1624, laundry was done indoors in new "bucking tubs" made by the cooper, John Alden. Then clothes were dried in front of the fireplace.

Mrs. Bradford had always cooked in a fireplace, because stoves had not yet been invented. The iron pots, griddles, and frying pans, hanging from hooks about the fireplace, were also familiar to her. But she knew nothing at first about how to prepare the strange New World foods.

74

Pilgrim meals centered around beans, squash, pumpkins, and especially corn. These were all dried, and had to be cooked several hours to make them tender. The women grew their own herbs, which they pounded with a mortar and pestle, to use for seasoning. The mortar and pestle could also be used for making cornmeal.

A usual breakfast was bean porridge reheated from the day before, and some hasty pudding. Hasty pudding was merely cornmeal boiled in water with molasses poured over it. It was served in a wooden porringer.

Leftover hasty pudding was set aside to cool and harden. At noon it was sliced and fried. It was served with stewed squash and fish

Herbs were placed in these cup-like mortars and then pounded with pestles into a powder. The mortar in the middle was brought to Plymouth on the *Mayflower*.

chowder, or succotash. Supper again was hasty pudding, with bean porridge that had cooked all day. Dessert was stewed pumpkins, simmered all day, sweetened with molasses, and flavored with ginger.

There was little meat, because the Pilgrims had no cattle. They had six goats, which gave milk for the babies. Their few chickens were saved to lay eggs. There were about 50 hogs and piglets. Enough of these were butchered in the fall to fill a hogshead for each household. Small pieces of the salt pork were used to flavor succotash and porridge. Like their seed corn, the Pilgrims' animals and chickens were carefully guarded so that there would be new ones the next year.

In the fall hunters brought home geese, ducks, and turkeys. Deer could be found all winter long. There were now 180 people in Plymouth, though, so there was rarely enough meat for everyone to have roast duck or venison steak. The deer and fowl were usually made into stews and soups, so there would be enough to go around.

The diet grew very tiresome, without any of what the Pilgrims called "comfortable things"— butter, cheese, wheat flour, spices, and sugar.

But the Pilgrims were grateful for the bountiful harvest that had filled every storehouse, proving that they were right in demanding separate farms. For the first time since they had arrived in Plymouth, there was always enough to go around throughout the winter.

The planters, as Governor Bradford said, were now "standing on their owne leggs."

This painting of Edward Winslow is the only known portrait of a *Mayflower* Pilgrim.

8. The First Taste of Sweetness

Edward Winslow returned from England in April of 1624, just as the Pilgrims had begun planting their crops. Their hearts were already high with hope. When the *Charity*, the same ship that had called in 1622, arrived with Winslow and his supplies, the atmosphere of Plymouth became much like that of a modern Christmas.

Eagerly the Pilgrims tore open the barrels and wooden chests, exclaiming joyfully over the contents. For the first time since they had come to Plymouth, they had new shoes and stockings! There was cloth, with scissors, needles, and thread to make new clothes.

For their homes, there were iron kettles, "spider" griddles with long spidery legs, rugs for their beds, and cotton yarn to make wicks for their oil lamps. Among the few "comfortable things" that Winslow had been able to buy were spices to make their food tastier, and salad oil.

Winslow had brought proper nets and hooks for fishing. He had brought the Pilgrims' first iron nails for building, and a good supply of saws, axes, hoes, spades, scythes, and reap-hooks—with files to keep the tools sharpened.

The first cattle had also arrived on the *Charity*—a bull and three heifers. Three cows could not provide enough milk for so many people, but the patient Pilgrims hoped that, in time, these cattle would breed others. Then there would be enough milk for every family.

Winslow brought a shipwright, too, who immediately set to work building boats. The Pilgrims needed them badly for trading and fishing. The unfortunate man had completed only two shallops, both of them a bit larger than the Pilgrims' old one, when he fell ill of a fever and died.

The men who had come on the *Anne* and
Little James now had been given farms.
Therefore the Pilgrims were able to plant twice
as much land in crops in 1624 as in the year
before. There were also more hands to help
with the labor. Again the crops were bountiful
and then at last, Governor Bradford said, the
Pilgrims "began to taste the sweetness of the
land."

"They began now highly to prize corn as
more precious than silver," he wrote. Those
who had corn to spare used it to buy small
items of clothing or household utensils from
other planters. Few Pilgrims had money, and
even if one did have, Governor Bradford said,
"corn was preferred before it."

The next year, everyone had some corn to
spare, and the Pilgrims made another trading
expedition among the Indians. This time, Governor Bradford proudly relates, they did not
take trinkets to barter with the Indians for
food to stay alive. Instead, they carried a
boatload of corn that they had grown themselves to trade for furs. They wanted to pay
their debts to the English merchants.

The men used one of their new shallops
to make the long, dangerous voyage to the

Kennebec River in Maine, home of the Abnaki Indians. They built a little deck across the middle of the boat to cover the corn and keep it dry. But the men, Governor Bradford said, "were faine to stand out all weathers without shelter."

Edward Winslow, who had been to Maine before, led the party safely to the mouth of the Kennebec River. There they found the Abnakis very happy to trade their furs for corn. These Indians liked to hunt and trap animals, but they did not like to farm. The trading party returned to Plymouth with 700 pounds of fine beaver, besides some other furs.

All of them were paid for, Governor Bradford said, with "this corn, which themselves had raised out of the earth."

Fur trading now became the Pilgrims' main business. They built a trading post on the Kennebec River, where the town of Augusta, Maine, now stands, and another at Aptuxcet, only 20 miles from Plymouth on Cape Cod. The trading posts were bigger and stronger buildings than the houses in Plymouth. Each had two large rooms with a fireplace in each room, and deep stone cellars underneath.

The trading posts were stocked with corn, and with English clothing and metal tools. The Indians had learned to like these better than their own skin garments and crude stone implements. Two agents stayed at each post the year around. Men from Plymouth took turns at these jobs, so no one had to stay away from home too long.

English ships now began to come to New England, bringing traders to buy furs from the Indians. These traders paid high prices to the Indians so that they could get a full cargo quickly and return home. Since the Pilgrims could not afford to pay as much, they were being driven out of the fur trade.

Then one summer day in 1627, a strange ship anchored at the Aptuxcet trading post. It was gaily decorated with flags and banners. Trumpeters sounded a fanfare, and a stout, richly dressed gentleman, surrounded by several attendants, came ashore. He was Isaac De Rasieres, secretary to Governor Peter Minuit of the new Dutch colony of New Amsterdam, now New York.

The visitor asked for Governor Bradford. The agents told him that Bradford was at Plymouth, a walk of six hours. The stout Dutchman sent

a messenger to Bradford, begging transportation. "I have not walked so far this three or four years, whereof I fear my feet will fail me," De Rasieres wrote.

Governor Bradford sent a shallop for De Rasieres. When the visitor arrived at Plymouth landing, the Governor, Elder Brewster, and other Pilgrim leaders were there to greet him. Captain Standish commanded a company of soldiers who fired a salute to welcome the Dutchman, then formed an honor guard to conduct him to Governor Bradford's house.

For this special occasion a scarlet rug was spread on the dirt floor of the first room. Mrs. Bradford prepared a fine meal for the visitor and the Pilgrim leaders.

After the meal, De Rasieres called to his attendants, who brought in several large chests. With great ceremony, De Rasieres opened the chests to show the Pilgrims his gifts to them. There were fine Dutch clothes, bolts of linen, and a chest of white sugar—the first the Pilgrims had seen since leaving England. In return, the Pilgrims presented the visitor with several hogsheads of tobacco, which they had bought from the Indians. An agreement was made for trade between the Pilgrims and the

Dutch, who wanted tobacco to ship to Holland.

Then De Rasieres brought out several strings of white and purple beads, made of periwinkle and quahog shells. This was *wampum*, he said, and the Hudson River Indian tribes treasured it above everything else. Perhaps the New England Indians would like it too.

The Pilgrims were skeptical, but they bought ten long strings out of courtesy to their visitor. De Rasieres was right. Wampum became so popular with the Indians that when trading they chose it over corn and even the English clothing that they liked so much. The Pilgrims alone knew where to get wampum, and soon they had won back the fur trade from the other Englishmen.

Wampum necklaces were popular trade items among the Indians who visited Pilgrim trading posts.

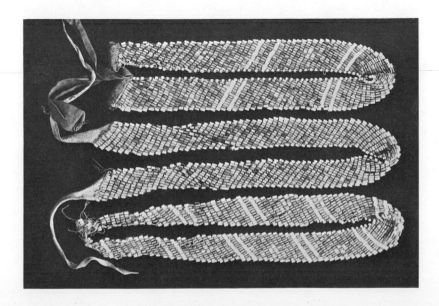

9. Mother Plymouth

On a September day in 1628, the Pilgrims' shallop sped northward to Massachusetts Bay. Aboard was a full cargo of corn and other supplies, and the Pilgrims' Dr. Samuel Fuller with his medicine chest.

A messenger had come to Plymouth from what is now Salem, Massachusetts, with a plea for help. A shipload of settlers from England had landed there to establish a new colony, but they were all sick.

Remembering their own sufferings upon landing in the wilderness almost eight years earlier, the Pilgrims sent all the medicines and "comfortable things" they could spare to their new neighbors.

Dr. Fuller stayed in Salem for six months. Little was known of medicine in those days, and we do not even know what disease the English settlers had. Dr. Fuller gave them medicines made of herbs, and bled them by cutting a vein in the arm to let a small amount of what was called "bad blood" drain out. In spite of his efforts, half of the Salem colonists died that winter.

Yet still more settlers came from England and more towns grew up in the new Massachusetts Bay Colony. Little Plymouth was the "mother" to them all. Elder Brewster and Dr. Fuller, who was also a deacon, taught them how to conduct their church services in the "Congregational Way" they used at Plymouth. And Governor Bradford, Edward Winslow, and others taught them how to govern themselves through the Town Meeting, with its free discussions and free elections.

These new neighbors were richer than the Pilgrims. They now had money and goods to

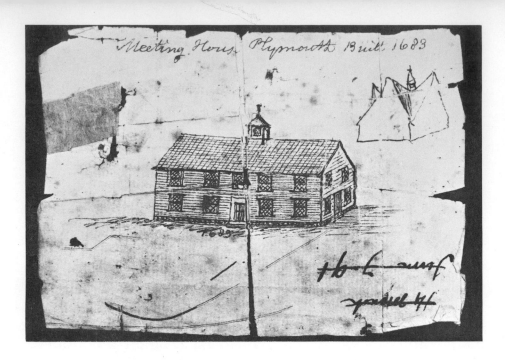

When the Pilgrims became more prosperous, they built a grander meeting house with diamond glass, a small cupola, and a bell.

exchange for all the corn, vegetables, and cattle that the Pilgrims could provide. Many Pilgrim families soon moved away from Mother Plymouth to find more land to farm, and to raise cattle. New towns were established that still exist today: Duxbury, Marshfield, Taunton, Sandwich, Barnstable, Yarmouth.

It saddened Governor Bradford to see that Plymouth was now almost a ghost town. Ships no longer came to little Plymouth harbor, but went to big, bustling Boston harbor. The Bay Colony also took away most of the Indian fur

90

trade. And finally, in 1691, the king of England made Plymouth a part of Massachusetts Bay Colony. After more than 70 years, Plymouth Colony was no more.

Governor Bradford did not live to bear this final blow. He died in 1657, after serving as governor for 32 years. His journal, the only complete record of Pilgrim history, was passed down in his family for three generations. Then it was placed in the library of the Old South Church in Boston. Few people ever read it.

During the American Revolution the British soldiers used Old South Church as a stable for their horses. After the war Governor Bradford's journal was missing from the library.

Also missing was his Letter-Book, in which Governor Bradford had kept copies of every letter he wrote or received. The Letter-Book was found a few years later in a grocer's shop in Halifax, Nova Scotia. Most of the letters were lost, because the grocer had used them for wrapping paper.

Generations passed. Americans knew that the Pilgrims had settled Plymouth Colony in 1620, but no one knew what they did there. Then, in 1855, a Massachusetts historian read some quotations about "Plimoth Plantation" in an English history book. He traced these quotations to an "anonymous" handwritten manuscript in the palace library of the Lord Bishop of London. It was Bradford's journal!

No one knows how it got to London. But the next year, 199 years after the death of the governor, *Of Plimoth Plantation*, by William Bradford, was published in Boston.

For the first time Americans learned the true story of how the Pilgrim Fathers stood alone against a vast wilderness, and conquered it.

Glossary

anonymous: written by a person whose name is unknown

barter: to pay for something with goods instead of with money

clout: a patch or piece of cloth used to mend something

communal: used or shared by all the members of a group

diplomat: a person who is skillful in dealing with other people

hogshead: a large barrel

mattock: a pickax-like tool used for loosening soil

musket: a long-barreled gun used before the rifle was invented

porridge: a food made of oatmeal or other cereal boiled in water or milk until thick

reaphook: a tool with a hook-shaped blade used to cut grain

rockweed: a seaweed which grows on rocks exposed at low tide

sapling: a young tree

shallop: a small, open boat with sails

succotash: a cooked food made of kernels of corn mixed with beans

treenails: wooden pins used to fasten together wooden boards

weir: a small dam in a river or stream

Index

A

Abnaki Indians, 83
Alden, John, 19, 27, 74
Allerton, Isaac, 49, 69

B

Boston Bay, 39
Bradford, Alice Southworth, 69
Bradford, Gov. William, 14, 21, 23, 24, 29, 36, 40, 41, 42, 43 (pic), 44, 49, 86, 90, 91, 92
Brewster, Ruling Elder William, 20, 29, 32, 35, 36

C

Canonicus, Chief, 21, 23
Cape Cod, 8
Chatham, 42
Children, 7, 16, 20, 33, 51, 52, 69, 70
Clothing, 30, 65, 72, 73
Cushman, Thomas, 28, 32, 33, 35, 36

D

De Rasieres, Isaac, 85–87

E

Education, 35, 36

England, 9

F

Farming, 46, 49, 50, 52, 54, 82
  communal system, 46, 49
  crops, 39, 40, 49, 56, 82
Fishing, 51, 52, 58–61
Food and Meals, 34, 38, 44, 61, 64, 65, 74, 75–77
France, 9
Fuller, Dr. Samuel, 31, 32, 36, 88
Fur trading, 84, 87

G

"General Sickness," 14, 20

H

Housekeeping, 70, 73, 74
Houses, 8–9 (pic), 17, 18, 19
  building of, 18 (pic), 19
  interior of, 69–72
Hunting, 62

I

Indians, 8, 40, 42, 43
  trade with, 40, 41 (pic), 42, 43, 44, 82, 83
  villages, 42, 43 (pic), 44

M

Massachusetts Bay Colony, 91
Massasoit, Chief, 23
Mayflower, 13 (pic)
Mayflower Compact, 21 (pic)
Monomoy, 42
Mullins, Priscilla, 20, 27

N

Narragansett Indians, 21, 23
Nauset, 42
Nemasket, 44

P

Plymouth, 22 (pic)
  Common House, 15
  defense of, 9, 10, 21–24, 26 (pic), 27 (pic)
  fort, 24, 26, 27 (pic)
  highway, 22 (pic)
  Street, The, 8
  wall, 23, 24

R

Religious services, 29–31 (pic), 32, 33, 36, 37

S

Ships, 41, 42, 43, 59, 80, 81 (pic)

Anne, 64
Charity, 39, 40
Discovery, 40
Fortune, 11, 12
Little James, 64
Mayflower, 13 (pic)
Swan, 39, 42, 43
Squanto, 21, 42, 51, 52, 56

Standish, Capt. Miles, 9, 24, 29, 67

T

Thanksgiving feast, 34–35 (pic)
Town Meeting, 48
Trading posts, 84, 85

V

Virginia, 12, 24, 39

W

Wampanoag Indians, 23
Wampum, 87 (pic)
Wessagusset, 39, 40, 42, 43
Winslow, Edward, 25, 38, 66, 78 (pic), 79, 80, 83
Women, 16, 37, 67, 68 (pic), 69